CW01316602

Third Revision

How I Went From Straight F's to Straight A's

Dr. Michael L. Jones

Copyright © 2023 Dr. Michael L. Jones.

All rights reserved. No part of this book may be used or reproduced by any means, graphic, electronic, or mechanical, including photocopying, recording, taping or by any information storage retrieval system without the written permission of the author except in the case of brief quotations embodied in critical articles and reviews.

This book is a work of non-fiction. Unless otherwise noted, the author and the publisher make no explicit guarantees as to the accuracy of the information contained in this book and in some cases, names of people and places have been altered to protect their privacy.

WestBow Press books may be ordered through booksellers or by contacting:

WestBow Press
A Division of Thomas Nelson & Zondervan
1663 Liberty Drive
Bloomington, IN 47403
www.westbowpress.com
844-714-3454

Because of the dynamic nature of the Internet, any web addresses or links contained in this book may have changed since publication and may no longer be valid. The views expressed in this work are solely those of the author and do not necessarily reflect the views of the publisher, and the publisher hereby disclaims any responsibility for them.

Scripture quotation are taken from THE HOLY BIBLE, NEW INTERNATIONAL VERSION®, NIV® Copyright © 1973, 1978, 1984, 2011 by Biblica, Inc.® Used by permission. All rights reserved worldwide.

ISBN: 978-1-6642-8900-0 (sc)
ISBN: 978-1-6642-8901-7 (hc)
ISBN: 978-1-6642-8899-7 (e)

Library of Congress Control Number: 2023900324

Print information available on the last page.

WestBow Press rev. date: 02/01/2023

Thanks To

Tom Reams
Loyd Haskins
Rick Burleson
Robby Butler

Contents

Introduction ix

Chapter 1   Rags to Riches 1
Chapter 2   Time to Share. 7
Chapter 3   A Tool 15
Chapter 4   Why it Works. 21
Chapter 5   A Rocky Start. 29
Chapter 6   "I Took Notes" 33
Chapter 7   The Method 45
Chapter 8   Tips 53
Chapter 9   The Fruits. 65
Chapter 10 Summary 71
Chapter 11 Build on the Basics 77

About the Book. 81
About the Author. 83

Introduction

Noah was a home-schooled sixteen-year-old. His father Dr. Arthur Robinson gave him a college-level physics book to learn with no outside help. Noah studied five to seven hours per day, but his error rate was 30%. He and his dad then read the booklet *The Overnight Student* and discovered a simple, new way of studying. Noah tried using this oral learning technique. His father said Noah started understanding the material better, and his study time was reduced, and his error rate fell to essentially zero.

After homeschooling, he passed enough advanced-placement exams to enter college as a junior. Whenever the material became too difficult, he employed his new study method, and he earned straight A's as a chemistry major. He applied for graduate school and took the Graduate Record Examinations. He used the study method to study for the GRE and received almost perfect scores. He was told by the Massachusetts Institute of Technology that he was their top pick. He ultimately chose Caltech for graduate school and graduated with a Ph.D. in chemistry in 3 years.

Jill White was the elementary principal of Christian Heritage Academy in Oklahoma City. A friend in Jill's Bible-study group said she had to take a week-long training and at the end of that week pass a banking examination as part of her job. She was nervous about it because she hadn't taken a test in years, and she had never been good at testing. So, Jill loaned her the booklet *The Overnight Student*. She quickly read it, applied it, and at the end of the week made the highest grade in the class.

How can something this simple be this powerful?

Chapter One
RAGS TO RICHES

Does this sound familiar? You're reading some material you really want to understand and remember. Perhaps it's the night before a test, and you're cramming. And you're telling yourself you'll never again wait until the last minute. And the clock is ticking. And you feel the adrenaline starting to flow.

That was me in the spring of 1969. To finance my schooling, I was working three part-time jobs. And I was under the additional pressure of being on academic probation because I had flunked out of the University of Oklahoma twice with two semesters in a row of straight F's. When you do that, you can't call yourself a student.

God must have felt sorry for me or just got tired of waiting for me to discover something that He knew was simple. I found myself getting up from my desk, not knowing for sure why I was getting up or what I was going to do, laying my notes on the bureau, and studying them in a way that was totally new to me.

Amazing things started happening. I was understanding difficult concepts quickly. I was remembering them. And I was actually having fun. Going from drudgery to fun was a pleasant surprise. I realized something new and strange was happening, and

I had possibly discovered something that was going to be life-changing.

Hit the Sack

My usual procedure was to stay up half the night, and I was prepared to do that. But before I knew it, I was through studying, and I knew that I knew the material. I went to bed with an excitement and a confidence that was new to me. When I walked into the classroom the next day, I couldn't wait to take the test.

My usual method of taking multiple-choice tests was to read the question, look at the possible answers, and eliminate the obviously wrong ones. But that usually left me with two choices. So, I would take my best guess. This time, as soon as I read the question, I knew the answer I was looking for. I found it, marked it, and zipped on to the next question. And for a change, I was one of the first to finish the test.

Miracle Time

When I received the results, I had made 100, and I wasn't even used to making A's. I was excited and couldn't wait to try my method on the next test. It was in a different subject, but I still made 100. In the next test in a still different subject, I made another 100.

That semester, I ended up making a 4.0 grade average with less effort than I had spent making bad grades.

I breezed through college with an effortlessness and a confidence that, in the past, I had thought was well beyond my abilities. I went on and earned a doctorate but never thought about sharing the technique.

Chapter Two

TIME TO SHARE

In 1989, I wrote a little twenty-page booklet describing the system. Shortly thereafter, I received a telephone call from a college instructor who had read a copy of the booklet. He had been in an automobile accident, and it had cost him his memory.

When he awoke in the hospital, a woman identified herself as his sister, but he didn't know what a sister was. A man identified himself as the doctor, but he didn't know what a doctor was.

He had lost his entire memory except for the use of the English language. He now faced the problem of how to earn a living, but he had lost all knowledge of his previous profession. However, as a college graduate, he was qualified to be a graduate teaching assistant.

He applied to his alma mater and was accepted. He used the technique in the booklet to learn the material and then walked into his classroom and taught the material without anyone knowing he had just learned it himself. He knew the university would not want to employ an instructor who had no knowledge of his subject.

Using a combination of courage, prayer, and the study system, he became an effective instructor and was popular with his students. He was enthusiastic about the study system and took the booklet to the department head and asked if he could share the technique with his students to help them in their studies. After reading the booklet, the department head gave his approval, and the instructor shared the booklet with his class.

The class became enthusiastic about the system, but there was only one booklet, so it was put on reserve in the college library. The students didn't want to wait their turn to check it out, so the instructor telephoned to ask if I could come and lecture his class.

Gulp

Only the night before, I had asked for prayer to help me overcome my fear of speaking in public. And now I was asked to speak to one of the toughest audiences of all — college students. They are bright, and they know it. I was afraid the average student in that class would be smarter than I was. There weren't too many students around who had failed every subject two semesters in a row. College students have inquiring minds and can quickly spot a phony. If they think a speaker is trying to con them, they'll tune him out. It was with many reservations that I said, "Okay."

The lecture was scheduled for a Friday afternoon. When I was in college, that was the time to cut classes, so I didn't expect many students to be there. Also, it was not a lecture they were going to be tested on. And it was a holiday weekend. Monday was Labor Day.

When I walked into that classroom, it was packed.

People were standing around the walls. There were students present who had come from other classes when they heard what the subject was going to be. And there were even some instructors. My primary thought as I delivered my talk wasn't to explain the learning system. It was to keep from passing out.

A Cool Reception

The technique I was explaining was so simple I was afraid they wouldn't take it seriously. At the conclusion of the lecture, I peered into faces searching for reactions, but all I saw were blanks. As they filed out, I felt maybe I had insulted their intelligence with a simple little technique they thought was foolish or had already figured out for themselves.

More Good Results

About a month later, I ran into the instructor in Oklahoma City. He said amazing things were happening with those students. They were coming into class asking questions that indicated a grasp of the subject beyond where they should have been at that point in their studies. They were making higher grades in that course than the students who didn't know the system, and they had improved their grades in their other courses. He said the other instructors wanted me to come and address *their* classes.

Later, I received a letter from the instructor. He said

every one of his sixty students told him they had raised their overall grade point average because of using the study system. He said he received phone calls from an assistant track coach and from an assistant baseball coach. They both said essentially the same thing: "I don't know what you're doing, but keep it up. Everyone in your class is making their grades."

A young lady, whose dream had been to become a medical doctor, had written the instructor saying the study system had boosted her grade average to the point where she felt confident in applying to medical school. So, she did, and she was accepted. Many of those original students reported that the study system changed the outcome of their student lives. One student had been failing, and his grandmother telephoned in tears and said, "I don't know what you did with my grandson, but he has decided to stay in school, and for the first time, he made his grades."

I was only a few days from moving to Washington State and didn't have time for a series of lectures. So, the head of the graduate teaching assistants suggested I give my lecture to the instructors while they videotaped it. They would then show the tape to their students and every year show it to their new students. So, that's what we did.

Out West

My first lecture in Washington was at Western Washington University. Two weeks later, I received a letter from Rick Burleson, one of the students. He wrote that the first time he used the method, he finished his test thirty minutes before the rest of the class and scored a perfect 100.

At semester's end, he wrote that he had missed a total of five questions on all the rest of the tests that semester, including final examinations and had made his first 4-point grade average. He said he was amazed he could sweat and struggle one semester and then easily receive a 4.0 the next. He was also pleased that not only were his classes easier, but now he had more free time.

Chapter Three

When you started elementary school, your teacher gave you a tool that helped you learn. You didn't like it much, but it worked pretty well. It was called homework. You learned by doing.

As you get older, teachers assign less and less homework. One day you find yourself in some classes in which the teachers assign no homework other than a reading assignment. She walks in, lectures, answers questions, gives you a reading assignment, and walks out. She repeats this for several weeks and then tests you on your knowledge of her lectures and the reading assignments.

When you reach this point in your student career, if your mind can quickly understand and remember her lectures and reading assignments, you don't need to worry about replacing the old tool with a new one. Otherwise, you are going to need a new tool.

When you've completed this book, you will have that new tool. And you'll be surprised at how simple and effective it is.

Where We Are

You and I, our parents, our teachers, and everybody

else were brought up in a system of education that presented us with information and then later tested us on that information. But what about in between — when we were all alone in our rooms trying to learn (understand and remember) that information?

Nobody really told us how to study the information. They told us to have a regular study place that was quiet and free of distractions. "Okay. Here I am. Now what?"

"Well, you know. Study. Read. Think." If the instructions at that point began to get a little vague, don't blame your teacher. Those were probably the same instructions she was given when she was a student. We were all in the same boat: sink or swim.

What if we began sinking while others around us were swimming? It's easy to start thinking maybe God shorted us in the brains department. That's a dangerous attitude because we tend to become the person we think we'll become. So much of a student's life is wrapped up in his success as a student that it colors his outlook on the rest of his life. It's hard to fully enjoy the fun things of life if you think you're dense, or if you feel guilty for not being at your desk studying for that upcoming test you know will be difficult.

Which Twin Are You?

Imagine two identical twins who are also identical in intelligence. In front of each one we place a board and a nail, and we give each twin the same instructions. "Get your nail into your board." But we give a hammer only to twin number one.

Twin number two will somehow find a way to get his nail in his board. He may turn his nail upside down and use the board as a hammer, or he may find a rock to drive the nail. His board and his nail are probably going to get damaged, and it's going to take him longer than it takes his twin.

Now, is he less intelligent than his brother? No, he just didn't have a tool. If he also had a hammer, he would have done just as good a job as his brother. If you are not as good a student as you would like to be, maybe nobody has ever given you a good tool.

Studying or Wandering?

If you're a normal student, you use what I call the 3-S system of studying. You Sit and Study Silently, and that's the hard way and the slow way. Too often, you just think you're studying, but what you're really doing is pronouncing words in your head while your mind has wandered off.

If someone would sneak up behind you, grab the book out of your hands, and ask you what you just read, you might not be able to tell him. Also, you are probably easily distracted. Your mind wanders onto things that are more interesting than the subject you're studying. You find yourself staring at objects in the room or listening to sounds. Sometimes, you may even fall asleep. You're about to receive a tool that makes those distractions impossible.

You don't need much training to operate a hammer, but it is a powerful tool that multiplies your effort. The study system you're about to learn is very similar to that hammer. It will fill the gap between the time your teacher presents you information and the time she tests you on that information. And it will definitely keep you from falling asleep. It will not only allow you to concentrate totally on your studies, but it will *force* you to concentrate, it will improve your understanding of the material, and it will greatly improve your retention.

That's a pretty tall order for a simple, little tool, but this simple, little tool is very powerful.

Chapter Four

You can ask any teacher, and you'll find one thing on which they all agree: the best way to learn something is to teach it. You never learn a subject as well as when you teach it to somebody else. Paul, in Romans 2:21, asks, "You then who teach others, do you not teach yourself?"

In 1985, the March/April issue of the Journal of Educational Research reported that three researchers from the University of Maryland and the U.S. Army Learning Resources Center performed an experiment on some North Carolina fourth graders. They gave each child the same written material to study by reading.

Then half the class reinforced their reading by illustrating it, while each member of the other half reinforced it by teaching it to another student. All students were then tested on their understanding and retention. Two days later, the students were tested again. The "teaching students" scored higher two days later than the "illustrating students" scored the first day!

In a lecture at Western Washington University in November of 1989, educator Robert Brand told us we remember only 14% of what we hear. We remember only 22% of what we both see and hear. We remember 70% of the movies in our mind. But we remember 91% of what we teach others.

That 91% figure is impressive. That will earn you an "A" on almost any test. But you say, "That's great for the teacher, but how does that help me?" When you use the tool you're about to receive, you become the teacher. "How can I teach something I don't know myself yet?" You do it the same way the little termite ate the big tree stump — one bite at a time, and you're about to learn how. "Who am I going to teach it to?" You're about to learn that too.

The Power of the Tongue

The Bible tells us about the power of the tongue — the powerful effect that spoken words can have on the person hearing them. We're told in Proverbs 18:21 that the tongue has the power of life and death. James 3:5 tells us: "The tongue is a small part of the body . . . but consider what a great forest is set on fire by a small spark."

As children, people told us that sticks and stones might break our bones, but words would never hurt us. Those bruises caused by sticks and stones will heal, but sometimes the bruises caused by careless words last forever. That's why we should be careful what we say to others because the power of the tongue is too great to be used carelessly.

Effect on Ourselves

Remember the old newsreels of Adolph Hitler making his arm-waving, lectern-pounding speeches? Do you think he could have turned tens of thousands of calm, cool, collected Germans into fanatics by handing them a handout or showing them some videos? He did it with the power of his tongue. Did you notice the effect his speeches had on himself? He turned himself into a wild-eyed fanatic because the power of the tongue also exerts itself on the person doing the talking.

That's why you should be careful of what you say about yourself. When you say, "I'll never be good at that," your words have an effect on you, and you probably never will be any good at "that." The system you're about to learn is going to direct the power of your tongue at yourself, but unlike Hitler, the power will be for good and not evil.

The Powerful Speaker

We've all seen public speakers who were truly dynamic and held us on the edge of our seats with their passionate, powerful delivery. If you ever secretly wished you could be that type of speaker, you can live your fantasy as you use this study technique.

Talking Is More Fun

Have you ever tried to have a conversation with someone who just wouldn't help? There were lots of awkward silences, and the conversation was strained and painful. You couldn't think of anything to say, and neither could he, and you were glad when it was over.

And then other times, the conversation was non-stop. You both were talking ninety miles per hour, each of you seemed to know what the other person was going to say, and it was so invigorating you hated to see it end.

Think about those good conversations. When was it the most fun — when you were doing the talking or the listening? It was when you were doing the talking. In fact, when you were doing the listening, you were probably just waiting for him to shut up so you could say what you had to say. With this study technique, you finally get to do all the talking.

No Pain, No Gain

Have you ever put weights on your wrists and ankles and then jogged or played a sport? When you removed the weights, you felt as if you could fly. While using this study system, you're going to put a burden on your mind that won't be there when you are taking your test; and the test will be easier than the studying.

Concentration

I've always suspected that the people who are the high achievers are the people who have the ability to totally concentrate on the task at hand and shut out all distractions. We tend to call these people brilliant when often, they are just good concentrators. One of the tests for mental competence is to see how long a person can concentrate on one thing before his mind wanders.

The Overnight Student

A reporter asked Barbara Nicklaus, wife of the champion golfer Jack Nicklaus, how she would describe her husband. The first thing that came to her mind was that he had intense concentration on most everything he did.

You're about to discover that you too can have that kind of concentration.

Chapter Five
A ROCKY START

I was certainly not an exceptional student in junior and senior high school. I made mostly B's and C's, and I was always thrilled with A's. However, I didn't see any reason why I couldn't succeed in college, and I enrolled at the University of Oklahoma.

Disaster

I struggled from day one, and one semester, my shortcomings caught up with me. I made an F in every subject — a zero-point grade average. According to the rules, they expelled me for one semester. Then, they allowed me to re-enroll on probation, and I promptly repeated my performance — straight F's. This time, they expelled me for two years. I think this was their way of saying, "Please don't come back."

Two years later, I asked the dean if he would re-admit me. He assigned some courses for me to take by correspondence and said if I averaged B's or better, he would re-admit me on probation. I gladly accepted because I knew with correspondence courses, I could spend as much time studying as I needed before taking the test.

I studied harder on those correspondence courses

than I had ever studied. I read every word. I underlined. I re-read. I re-underlined. I didn't take the tests until I knew I was ready. Under those conditions, I was able to attain the B average, but I suspected that back in school, I would be in trouble again. In addition to being a full-time student, I was going to have to work to finance my schooling.

Another Chance

Back in school, I tried as hard as I could. When I wasn't eating, sleeping, working, or in class, I was studying. I almost wore out my books with reading, underlining, and re-reading. My social life was zero, and I constantly felt pressure. All around me, I could see students making better grades with less effort. I just assumed God had given them more brains. It didn't occur to me that maybe I was just lacking a simple tool.

One night, I visited a girl who lived at home with her mother, and her mother made the comment I was tired of hearing. "I always made good grades, and I hardly cracked a book." I swallowed my pride and asked her how she did that. She answered, "I took notes."

Chapter Six

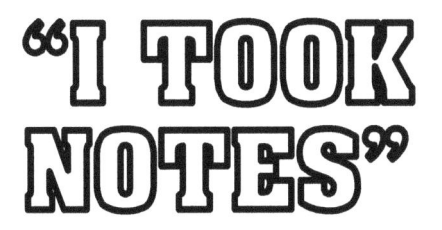

"I TOOK NOTES"

I thought about that answer, but it couldn't be that simple. That was too easy. Besides, I already took notes, or I thought I took notes, or at least, I took notes when I went to class and when I wasn't daydreaming. When I thought about it, I was really a pretty haphazard note-taker because I always knew I could get it from the textbook.

Textbooks

Let me tell you something about those textbooks. The people who write them know their subjects. But Don and Katie Fortune revealed in their excellent book *Discover Your God-given Gifts* that only six percent of people have "teaching" for their strongest aptitude. That means about sixteen out of seventeen knowledgeable, well-meaning people who write textbooks are probably not too good at explaining things to others. In fact, the better an author knows his subject, the more difficult it often is for him to explain it to you. He will tend to leave things out because they are so obvious to him that he assumes they are obvious to you.

On February 15, 1990, I was in my car listening to KNTR Radio in Ferndale, Washington. It was an interview with a lady who described herself as a lay person — not a scholar. She and some other non-scholars had obtained some textbooks that had passed all editing and inspection requirements and were certified error-free and ready for the classroom. These non-scholars found so many errors that they quit counting individual errors and began counting pages of errors.

One historical date was off by 60 years. One author attributed an incident in the life of one of our U.S. presidents to the wrong president. Another author gave incorrect geographical information.

Should we be upset with these authors? Maybe a little, but they have held themselves out as experts — not teachers. Asking a non-teacher to teach is like asking a tone-deaf person to sing.

Use Your Teacher

So, what's the answer? For you, the answer is to rely less on the textbook and more on the teacher. You can't ask questions of your textbook, but you can ask questions of your teacher. She can fill in the gaps, and she can give you examples to explain the concepts. She knows you better than that author knows you, and she can talk on your level. If she's really good, she can sense if you really understand or if you're just nodding your head.

When a teacher walks into a classroom, she's not thinking, "What shall I talk about today?" Ten minutes later, she's not thinking, "I'm bored with this. I think I'll talk about something else." She knows what she's going to talk about, she knows the order in which she's going to present it, and she's going to try hard not to mention words or concepts she hasn't already explained. Unless God blessed you with total recall, there is only one way you can take advantage of the work your teacher has done for you, and that is for you to take good notes.

A New Attitude

So, I decided I would take good notes because I would much rather study my notes than those textbooks. I went to each of my instructors and asked, "Will you ever test us on material you haven't covered in class?" They all said, "No." And some seemed offended I would suggest such a thing. Great! That was just what I wanted to hear.

From that point on, I assumed there was no such thing as a textbook, and the only information I was going to get was what the teacher said and what I wrote in my notes. That attitude forces you to pay attention in class.

Return on Investment

If there was a machine that, for every dollar you put in, would give you five dollars back, you'd think that was worth the trouble. That's a good return on investment. Taking notes is just that type of investment. For every hour you spend taking good notes, you will save several hours outside of class trying to figure out what the teacher was explaining, what the textbook is trying to explain, what the other students seem to know, and what you need to know to do well on the test.

Let's Take Notes

Here's the basics for taking notes. First, you must go to every class. You arrive on time. You should sit on the front row or as close as you can to the front row. You have your pen and paper (or fingers and keyboard) ready, so you can start writing when the teacher starts talking.

You've been taught how to outline:

   1.
      A.
         (1.)
            (a.)

This is the best way to take notes. If you walk into biology class, and the teacher says, "We're going to learn about birds today," you write:

   Birds

Then, she says she's first going to talk about carnivorous birds. Your notes now read:

   Birds
      1. Carnivorous

Then, she says the first carnivorous birds she will discuss are hawks.

    Birds
        1. Carnivorous
            A. Hawks

Then, she says the first hawk she will discuss is the Red-tailed Hawk.

    Birds
        1. Carnivorous
            A. Hawks
                (1.) Red-tailed Hawk

See how much better this is than:

    Birds, Carnivorous, Hawks, Red-tailed Hawk
    or
    Birds
    Carnivorous
    Hawks
    Red-tailed Hawk

If your notes are well-organized at the end of class, the battle is half won. Even if you leave the outline symbols out, simple indenting is a great help in seeing the relationship between items. Understanding those relationships is a great help in understanding and remembering. Even though the class was only an hour long, the student who spent the hour daydreaming, whispering, passing notes, and doodling is more than an hour behind you.

Mind Reading?

Teachers get pretty good at teaching, especially when they teach the same subject over and over. There is one thing they never get good at — reading minds. If she is going too fast for you to take notes, she has no way of knowing it unless you let her know. You're going to have to get your hand in the air and ask her to repeat. Until you do, she has every right to assume you're keeping up.

If she says something you don't understand, she has no way of knowing unless you let her know. You're going to have to get your hand in the air and ask her to explain. Until you do, she is going to assume you are understanding everything she is saying. You're probably not the only one who didn't understand. Too embarrassed? Ask her after class.

The Wandering Mind

Did you know that, in any audience, at any point in time, there are people who are not listening even if they are interested in the topic? Should you be embarrassed when you discover you haven't been listening? No, that just means you're normal. We are all made that way. We can keep our mind on one subject for only so long, and there are other things that are much more interesting to think about. I'm sure the same thing happens to teachers when they attend teachers' meetings.

What do you do when you discover your mind has drifted, and you missed that last thing the teacher said? A good teacher would already have emphasized that it's okay to ask her to repeat something. So, you get your hand in the air and ask her to repeat.

What do you do when you realize you haven't been listening for several minutes? You don't ask the teacher to repeat that much information. You can't ask your neighbor because you shouldn't be talking, and you would be interfering with his listening to the teacher, and you both would be missing the teacher's *new* information.

You leave a gap in your notes — a large gap. If three minutes of lecture would normally occupy a quarter of a page in your notebook, leave a half page blank. Now that you've returned to earth, start taking notes again.

No Gaps

At the conclusion of class, you hustle up to the teacher and find out what you missed; or, if you have a classmate who's a good note-taker, you get the information from him. You never leave that gap in your notes. The missing information can make all the difference in you understanding the information that follows.

If you had to leave a gap in your notes during the biology lecture on birds, and when you started writing again, the teacher was saying, "... and this bird is rarely seen in daytime and mainly hunts at night," you'll probably think that doesn't sound like a hawk. When you talk with the teacher after class, you find out she had switched the topic to owls, and now things make sense.

You're Not Alone

Why don't students raise their hands when they miss something or don't understand something? It's because they are afraid they are the only one so afflicted, and they will look foolish in front of their classmates. The next time you feel that way, stick up your hand and ask your question.

While the teacher is answering your question, look around and see how many of your classmates are writing down the information she's giving you. I think you'll discover a lot of your fellow students are glad you asked that question.

Thou Shalt Not

If you ever find yourself on the other side of that fence, and one of your classmates asks a question that you think is foolish, don't ever do anything that would let him or anyone else know that you think his question is silly. He may ask a question that the teacher just answered a few minutes ago, or it may be a simple fact that everybody else knows.

If you let it be known that you think his question

is silly, how do you think that's going to make him feel? Do you think he'll ask any more questions if he's afraid you're going to make him look foolish in front of the class? Do you think anyone else who is afraid their question might be silly is going to ask it and take a chance the class might laugh or roll their eyes? In Proverbs 6:19, that's called "stirring up dissension." This is also known as enmity, and the Bible calls it one of the worst sins.

Thou Shalt

Your note-taking skills will develop rapidly. You'll invent your own abbreviations that won't mean anything to anyone else, but that's okay. They only have to be meaningful to you. At the conclusion of class, you should feel as if you need to shake the cramps out of your fingers. You should feel as if you've put in a hard fifty minutes, and you need that ten-minute break between classes.

On the days when the teacher gives a well-prepared, well-organized lecture, and when you do a good job of taking notes, you'll feel as if you already know the material and could probably be tested on it right then.

I don't like to take notes. But I would rather spend one hour taking notes than spend several agonizing hours trying to learn the material from a textbook. I'm sure you'll agree.

Is note-taking a new idea? Hardly. Over 3400 years ago, Moses told his people, in Deuteronomy 6:9, to write the Ten Commandments as an aid to learning them.

Chapter Seven
THE METHOD

If you are expecting a complicated study system that will take time and practice to master, you're in for a surprise. You can apply this one as soon as you lay this book down.

Take a Bite

Now, stand up. The October 1989 issue of Readers Digest reported in their "News from the World of Science" section that we think five to twenty percent faster when standing.

Take your notes, or your book, or whatever your source document is, and lay it where you can easily refer to it like the student on the cover of this book is doing. Isaiah 28:10 of the King James Version tells us that teaching is by precept on precept, line on line, here a little and there a little. So, pick the first bite-size portion, perhaps a paragraph, and read it. Now, turn away from your notes.

Use Your Tongue

Now, teach what you just read, *out loud, using your own words*, to an imaginary class. Don't talk in a monotone. Vary your voice inflection. Use your hands. Be a teacher.

Here is what is probably going to happen when you first try this. You're going to get "tongue-lock." You're going to stand there, and nothing is going to come out of your mouth. Now you'll begin to realize what happened to you those times when you thought you had studied, and you thought you knew the material; and then, when you went in to take the test, you couldn't think of the answer. Have you ever said, "I know it. I just can't explain it?" You were probably kidding yourself.

Read your bite-size portion again. This time, decide how you are going to explain it to your class in your own words and using your own examples. Your mind works differently when you read something with the intention of explaining it to someone else. Nobody wants to look silly in front of an audience and not know what he's talking about.

Stage Fright

Something else that sometimes happens is strange indeed. If you get nervous speaking in front of people, you're going to get nervous. Even though your audience is imaginary, and you are all alone in your room, you're going to feel a little stage fright. It will pass.

Light Bulbs

As you overcome these startup phenomena, you're going to experience something else quite strange — especially if you are studying a subject that has been difficult for you. You're going to start thinking, "Now I see what that teacher was trying to say. Why didn't she just say that?"

Well, she probably did say that. She might have said it several times in several different ways, but you were just listening then, and that's 14% retention. Now you're teaching, and that's 91% retention. Things are starting to come together, light bulbs are coming on, and you're starting to understand both the forest and the trees.

Let's say you're studying for a U.S. geography test, and the first sentence reads, "The four states that border with Mexico from west to east are California, Arizona, New Mexico, and Texas." That's a pretty small bite, but we'll use that for our illustration.

You turn to your class and say something along these lines: "Okay class. Out of all fifty states, only four touch Mexico's border. From left to right, the first one is California, and you would expect it to be because to the left of California is the ocean."

Where did all that stuff come from? Nothing like that was in your notes. That stuff came from your imagination as you were just being yourself and using your own words and your own examples. Never mind if it sounds silly. This is your show.

Don't Be a Parrot

If all you do is turn around and repeat verbatim what your notes say, you are not teaching. You are memorizing. You are parroting. You are a recording playing through a speaker. Parrots and recorders don't understand. They just repeat. Parroting information is useless to you because it doesn't increase your understanding, and it doesn't increase your retention.

When you parrot your notes, the information in your notes will shortly leave your head and go back to your notes. But when you use your own words and your own examples, that information is becoming part of you. Did you get that? Your own words and your own examples.

The Dreaded Blank

Now you are continuing to teach your geography class. "The next state to the east of California that touches Mexico is Arizona, and that makes sense because Mexico is a desert country, and Arizona is a desert state. " You're starting to have fun with your imagination, but let's say your mind goes blank at this point; and you can't remember the next state. You go back to your notes and find that New Mexico is the next state and is followed by Texas.

You turn back to your class and say, "Okay class. Out of all fifty states . . ." Notice that you start over from the beginning of your bite-size portion. That's important. If you had started over with the state you forgot — New Mexico — you would probably forget it next time too.

Your mind works best when it works in sequence from one thing to the next to the next. Even computers work best that way. Your computer can give you information faster if you ask for it in the same order in which the information was put in.

Momentum

When you start your mind going along a sequence that it has been along before, it will tend to keep going all by itself. A television interviewer once asked me a question that required an answer from my lecture. I had given that lecture so many times that my answer set in motion the next point. Before I could stop myself, I was giving my lecture, and the interviewer had to break in to shut me up.

Go ahead and refer to your notes as often as you need until you can teach your bite-size portion a few times without referring to your notes. You're going to be surprised how quickly you'll be able to do that.

Take Another Bite

Now, pick your next bite-size portion, and repeat the procedure. You continue in this fashion until you reach the end of your notes. It's not necessary that you be able to teach your entire notes from memory without referring back to them, but it is necessary that you be able to teach each bite-size portion from memory.

How many times do you go back to the start of your notes and run through the routine? You won't know the answer to that until you get to the end of your notes. How confident do you feel? How important is the test? You be the judge, but keep in mind that the more times you run through it, the better you will know it. Also, every time you go through the routine, the faster it goes.

Chapter Eight
TIPS

There is no reason for you to learn things the hard way when I've done that for you. The following suggestions will allow you to quickly and easily get good results from your new tool.

Alone

This technique works best if you are alone — especially at first. You would be too distracting to another person, and they would be too inhibiting to you.

Up and at 'Em

After standing up and picking your bite-size portion, turn and teach it while you are moving around. You can pace back and forth. You're going to be surprised how accelerating your body will accelerate your mind. Your concentration will be more focused, and distractions will start fading away. Some people instinctively start pacing when trying to solve a particularly difficult problem.

Mums the Word

When you first start using your new tool, don't tell anybody about it. Just do it. You should not take the chance of running into Mr. Negative. He can find the bad in any situation. When you tell him about your idea for a wonderful, new invention, he says. "Nah, that'll never work." When you tell him about Susan's party you're going to, he says, "I heard those were boring."

The power of the tongue is strong whether it speaks a lie or the truth. If he says something negative about your new study tool, his words will affect you whether you realize it or not. You don't need to hear negative words — especially when trying something new which is when you're most vulnerable. Just use the technique, and after it's working for you, then talk about it. You should share it with others, and no one will be able to throw a wet blanket on you when you are experiencing success.

GIGO

Computer people have a saying: GIGO. Garbage In Garbage Out. If you put bad information into your computer, you're going to get bad information out. What this means to you is that the better your notes are, the better your studying will be.

Motor Mouth

I found that if I would talk fast, it forced me to concentrate better and to think faster. Also, it was more fun, I had to know the information better in order to talk fast, and I would get through studying more quickly.

Improvise

Don't be afraid to experiment with this system to adapt it to different classes or study environments. For example, if you're studying for a math test, it's inconvenient to work a problem while you're walking around. If you have access to a chalkboard or a whiteboard, you can work out the problem on the board while you explain to your class what you're doing and why you're doing it. If you don't have a board, work the problem on a sheet of paper and explain what you're doing while your imaginary class looks over your shoulder.

If you're studying for a laboratory test, imagine yourself and your class in the lab with all the necessary lab equipment. Go through the motions with your hands as you teach your class. If you perform the experiments in your imagination, they will go more smoothly during the exam.

When those first college students I lectured to were studying for the same test, they would get together and practice on each other. One would be the teacher while the other would be the student, and then they would switch roles. This is better than the old 3-S system, but each student gets to be the teacher only half the time. The other half, they are just listening, and that's just 14% retention. If the student would use this tool by himself, he would be the teacher all the time, and that's 91% retention.

What do you do if you're studying for a test in study hall where you're supposed to be quiet? You can't get up and walk around jabbering, so you do the next best thing. You sit by yourself, you read your bite-size portion, you cover it with something, and you explain it to your class in your mind. If possible, sit by yourself, so you can speak quietly enough that only you can hear. Talking works better than imagining.

You can experiment all you want with this study system, but there is one thing you must never change: *teaching out loud.* In my twenty-three years of attending schools, I've never found a more simple and powerful technique for learning.

Just Imagine

Your imagination is not only fun to use, it is a very powerful learning tool. God likes to teach us by inserting visions into our dreams. Do you realize that everything starts with a vision?

If you buy a piece of land and call an architect and tell him to go look at it and design a house to fit it, he'll drive over and before he even gets out of his car, he'll be visualizing your house. He'll stand there thinking, "Let's put the garage over there and the living area over there and the deck over there." Then he'll take out a note pad, sketch a rough design, drive back to his office, and start adding details. Eventually, there's the house on your land.

Where was the first image of that house? It wasn't on the architect's pad. It was in his mind when he first looked at the property. Remember, we said we remember 70% of the movies in our mind. Those are the movies you create in your mind using your imagination.

The next time you're studying a history lesson, use your imagination and take your class with you to that moment in time. If you're studying a battle, point out to your class the horses coming over the horizon, see the sun rays shining through the dust they kick up, hear the bullets whiz by, feel the ground shake and the grit in your eyes and teeth, and see and smell the gun smoke. Some history can be exciting when you look beyond the words on the page and insert yourself into the scene.

Memory Tricks

Here's where your imagination can do some amazing things. Go to most bookstores, and you'll find some books on how to improve your memory. If you look through them, you'll probably find these two little jewels which are simple but powerful. If you don't know them, it's time.

I'm going to describe some things to you. As you read these words, use your imagination, and create a three-dimensional movie in your mind. The more of your senses you use — color, movement, sound, smell, touch — the better you'll remember. Here we go.

You hear a noise in your utility room. You investigate, and it's the washing machine, and it is agitating. (Hear it? See it vibrate?) There is a skinny man with a very big Adam's apple standing on it. The man is not moving, but his Adam's apple is bouncing up and down. (See it?) On his head is a black tomcat that is gripping the man's head with all of its claws. (See it?) When it sees you, it gets mad, bears its teeth, and hisses at you. (See it? Hear it?)

What you have just quickly done, in probably less time than it would have taken you otherwise, is memorize the first four presidents of our country. The WASHING machine reminds you of George WASHINGton. The bouncing ADAM'S apple reminds you of John ADAMS. The TOMcat reminds you of THOMAS Jefferson. The MAD cat reminds you of James MADison.

There is no limit to the number of articles you can stack on top of each other to remind you of whatever it is you want to remember. The key is to imagine a vivid connection between the top of one object and the bottom of the next as the mad cat gripping the head. However, if you stacked twenty objects in your mind to remind you of twenty things, and you quickly needed to know what the ninth item was, you would have to start at the bottom and replay the scenario and work your way back up.

Memory Trick Two

There is another system that will allow you to instantly

go to the ninth item, or the ninety-ninth. On a piece of paper, write in a column the numbers one through ten, or if you're ambitious, one through one hundred. Pick a word that rhymes with each number and write it beside its number. For the number "one," you might choose "sun" or "gun". For "two," you might choose "zoo" or "shoe." "Three" could be "sea" or "tree." Memorize which word goes with which number. For the rest of your life, those are your words that go with those numbers.

Now, let's say you are going to memorize every U.S. president and the number of his presidency. Let's say that, for the number thirty-two, you had chosen the words, "dirty shoe." When you get to the thirty-second president, you find it was Franklin D. Roosevelt. When I think of Franklin D. Roosevelt, I always remember those pictures of him with that big toothy grin and that cigarette holder he often had clenched between his teeth.

So, I'm going to visualize me bending over and starting to put on a dirty, jogging shoe. Then, somebody's hand grabs my shoe. I look up, and there stands Franklin D. Roosevelt with that big toothy grin on his face and a cigarette holder clenched between his teeth. He jams the shoe into the cigarette holder, lights it, and smokes it. Pretty bizarre, huh? The more bizarre it is, the better I'll remember it.

Now, when someone asks me who the thirty-second president was, I'm going to think of thirty-two which reminds me of dirty shoe which reminds me of my starting to put it on, someone grabbing it, my looking up, and seeing FDR grinning and smoking it. Or, if someone asks which president Franklin D. Roosevelt was, I'll see him smoking that dirty shoe which I know stands for thirty-two.

Let me caution you against using a memory device as a crutch when you are unable to understand something. Remember, parrots can memorize.

Every Night

Once you're comfortable with this study technique, Mr. Procrastination will tempt you to wait until the night before the test to study. That is not a good practice because of the possibility of an error in your notes. You might have written "positive" instead of "negative," or maybe the teacher was distracted and said positive instead of negative. You notice, while you're studying, that positive doesn't make sense, but it's too late to ask the teacher because the test is the next day. You may not have an opportunity to get with the teacher before test time.

The ideal practice is to use this technique each night to cover the information given you that day as if you were going to be tested on it the next day. Your classmates and teacher will be surprised at the intelligent questions you'll come up with, and you'll be surprised at how well you will understand each new day's lecture and how much easier taking notes becomes.

Where's my "A"?

What if you dutifully follow all these steps and suggestions and still can't make an "A"? You should consider the strong possibility that you are taking a subject that requires an aptitude that you don't have. God didn't give everybody the same package of talents.

Economics has always been a fuzzy subject for me, but I think, using this system, I could make an A in it. But if I don't make an A, my attitude should be the same as yours should be. Big deal! I just won't make it my life's work.

Anytime, Anywhere

Moses accepted the responsibility of teaching the commandments to the people. What did he tell them to do in order to learn the commandments? In Deuteronomy 6:7, he tells the people to teach the commandments and to talk about them. He said to talk about them when you get out of bed, when you sit in your house, when you walk along the road, and when you go to bed. When he said to talk about them, we assume he meant with other people, but that's not necessary. We don't need other people around if we want to talk out loud about something.

If you've learned the material by teaching out loud, you can review it any time even if you don't have your notes — while walking, jogging, driving, etc. If you would be disturbing other people, teach your class in your mind.

Several weeks after lecturing at King's High School in Seattle, the principal told me that one of her teachers had noticed a student walking down the hall talking to himself. When the teacher asked him what he was doing, he said, "I'm teaching my class."

Chapter Nine
THE FRUITS

The Bible tells us to judge things by their fruits, so here are some tasty ones.

New Eyes

One of the biggest fruits of this system touched me so much that I still remember where I was when it happened, even though it was fifty years ago.

I was on the north side of the street walking west a half block from leaving the campus when I realized, "This is no fluke. I can repeat this. I can make an A in almost anything I want to make an A in. And without killing myself." It was as if a heavy dark cloud that had weighed me down for ten years suddenly lifted off and disappeared. I began noticing things I had been blind to: the beauty of nature, the joy of friendly people, the visions of a future, happy life.

Jesus didn't tell us in John 10:10 that he came so life would be *less* full. He came so it would be *more* full. If our life isn't full, it isn't Jesus' fault. He did his part.

Dr. Michael L. Jones

Essay Questions

The reason most students have trouble with essay tests is because their attempt to answer the essay question is their first attempt to put all those facts together in their own words. When you study by teaching out loud, you're getting lots of practice doing exactly that. You'll find you can often give the teacher more than she wants.

Final Exams

I always hated finals because I had to re-cram information that I hadn't learned well the first time. This time however, when I laid all my past-semester's notes down, and when I started at the beginning, I would remember the words and examples I had used earlier in the semester to teach this information to my "class." Before I knew it, I was through studying.

While other students were up half the night studying, I would be sleeping the good sleep. I would go in and make A's on all my finals, while other students, who were probably smarter, had to work harder to make their A's because they didn't have the tool I had.

Gifted?

I always worried that I had nothing to offer the

The Bible tells us to judge things by their fruits, so here are some tasty ones.

New Eyes

One of the biggest fruits of this system touched me so much that I still remember where I was when it happened, even though it was fifty years ago.

I was on the north side of the street walking west a half block from leaving the campus when I realized, "This is no fluke. I can repeat this. I can make an A in almost anything I want to make an A in. And without killing myself." It was as if a heavy dark cloud that had weighed me down for ten years suddenly lifted off and disappeared. I began noticing things I had been blind to: the beauty of nature, the joy of friendly people, the visions of a future, happy life.

Jesus didn't tell us in John 10:10 that he came so life would be *less* full. He came so it would be *more* full. If our life isn't full, it isn't Jesus' fault. He did his part.

Essay Questions

The reason most students have trouble with essay tests is because their attempt to answer the essay question is their first attempt to put all those facts together in their own words. When you study by teaching out loud, you're getting lots of practice doing exactly that. You'll find you can often give the teacher more than she wants.

Final Exams

I always hated finals because I had to re-cram information that I hadn't learned well the first time. This time however, when I laid all my past-semester's notes down, and when I started at the beginning, I would remember the words and examples I had used earlier in the semester to teach this information to my "class." Before I knew it, I was through studying.

While other students were up half the night studying, I would be sleeping the good sleep. I would go in and make A's on all my finals, while other students, who were probably smarter, had to work harder to make their A's because they didn't have the tool I had.

Gifted?

I always worried that I had nothing to offer the

gifted student, but I've always suspected that some gifted students are just gifted with good memories.

Once, while giving my lecture, a gifted student started getting excited and was saying, "Yeah. Yeah." His friends around him asked what he was getting excited about, since he already made good grades.

He came up to me after the lecture and said he had a good memory, and that allowed him to make good grades. He said he could often remember where on the textbook page the information was. He admitted that sometimes he didn't really understand the material. He said he could see how studying this way would improve his understanding.

Even if you're a gifted student, I think you'll find that, studying this way, you'll understand the material better, you'll enjoy studying more, you'll get through studying more quickly, and you'll remember the information longer.

Not So Bad After All

Everyone has subjects they don't like. As you learn more about a subject, you'll probably find that you are becoming more interested in it, and maybe it isn't so bad after all. Lack of understanding is usually the culprit behind our dislike of something — or somebody.

The Business World

Don't leave this learning technique behind when you

leave school and enter the work force. The employee who gets the raises and promotions is usually the guy who knows without having to ask or look up the information. "Ask Joe. He always knows." Well, Joe is the guy who's on his way up the organization.

Management level businessmen can get buried in new information they must know just to maintain their current position — never mind getting ahead. They could use a way of quickly understanding and remembering, so they don't have to stop and search through reference material or ask someone else.

Chapter Ten

SUMMARY

Remember the burden we said would be on your mind when you studied that would not be there when you were taking the test? It's harder to recall facts when you're speaking to an audience than when you're writing on a piece of paper. And this is true even if your audience is imaginary. Also, if you studied using the motor-mouth technique, that technique requires a quicker grasp of facts than does marking an answer on the answer sheet.

Remember the dynamic public speaker? If you envied him, go ahead and ham it up while you're teaching.

Remember the concentration that is so valuable but so elusive? It's almost impossible for your mind to wander while you're teaching a class — especially if you're also walking around.

When you're starting something new, it's nice to have a clear track on which to run, so here are your recipes:

Taking Notes

1. Assume no textbooks
2. Attend every class
3. On time
4. Front row is best
5. Pen and paper (or fingers & keyboard) ready

6. Use outline form
7. If teacher talks too fast, ask her to repeat — now or after class
8. If teacher says something you don't understand, ask her to explain — now or after class
9. If your mind wanders for a few seconds, ask her to repeat — now or after class
10. If your mind wanders for a longer period, leave a gap in your notes, and fill in after class

Study

1. Stand up
2. Read bite-size portion
3. Turn away from notes
4. Move around
5. Teach out loud (MOST IMPORTANT OF ALL)
6. Use your own words
7. Use your own examples
8. Refer to notes until you can teach a few times without referring to them.
9. Choose next bite-size portion
10. Repeat

Tips

1. Mums
2. GIGO
3. Alone
4. STAND UP and move around (hot tip)

5. Use imagination
6. Motor mouth
7. Use nightly

Super Summary

There are about 11,000 words in this book. I've always thought a speaker should be able to summarize the main point of his speech in a few words. If you remember nothing else from this book, remember these six words when you study:
STAND UP AND TEACH OUT LOUD.

Chapter Eleven
BUILD ON THE BASICS

I don't care what your goal in life is. If you start out by getting really good at the basics, everything else will be easier.

The 1958 Green Bay Packers were the worst team in Packer history having won only one game. The next year, Vince Lombardi took over coaching duties and drilled his players over and over on the two basics of football: blocking and tackling. If all the blockers do their job, you make a touchdown every time. If all the tacklers do their job, the other team never makes a touchdown.

In Lombardi's first year, the Packers jumped to 7–5, and he was named Coach of the Year. The next year, the Packers won their conference championship for the first time in sixteen years. Then, they went on to win their next nine post-season games — a record at the time. Under Lombardi, they won five titles and won the first two Super Bowls.

You have now been given the basics of learning — the blocking and tackling of learning — **IN ONLY SIX WORDS**. This will work for you, and when it does, you're going to feel thankful. James 1:17 tells us that every good and perfect gift is from above, coming down from the Father. That verse doesn't say *some* good gifts. It says *every* good gift, and any gift that has been life-changing for virtually everyone who has used it is a good gift. So, now you know who to thank.

About the Book

Every teacher agrees the best way to learn something is to teach it. Is there some way a student can take advantage of this principle? He wants to learn, but he can't teach something he doesn't know yet. Or can he? In this short, easy-to-read book, you will be given a simple method of studying that has quickly worked for everyone who has used it. You will surprise yourself at how quickly you understand and remember the material.

About the Author

Mike Jones grew up in a small Oklahoma town. He was an average high school student but a terrible college student. After two semesters in a row of straight F's, he was re-admitted on probation. One night while frantically studying for a test, he was inspired to try a new study method. He quickly started understanding and remembering the information and was actually having fun. The next day, he made 100 on the test. Then on the next test -- another 100. And on the next -- another 100. And then his first 4.0. Then on to a bachelor's degree. Then on to a doctorate.

Universities, high schools, middle schools, and even elementary schools have requested his results-generating lectures including non-denominational, Christian, and Catholic Schools. He has lectured on radio, television, in churches, and even on a ship.